Nifty

For Crayons and Wide Tipped Markers

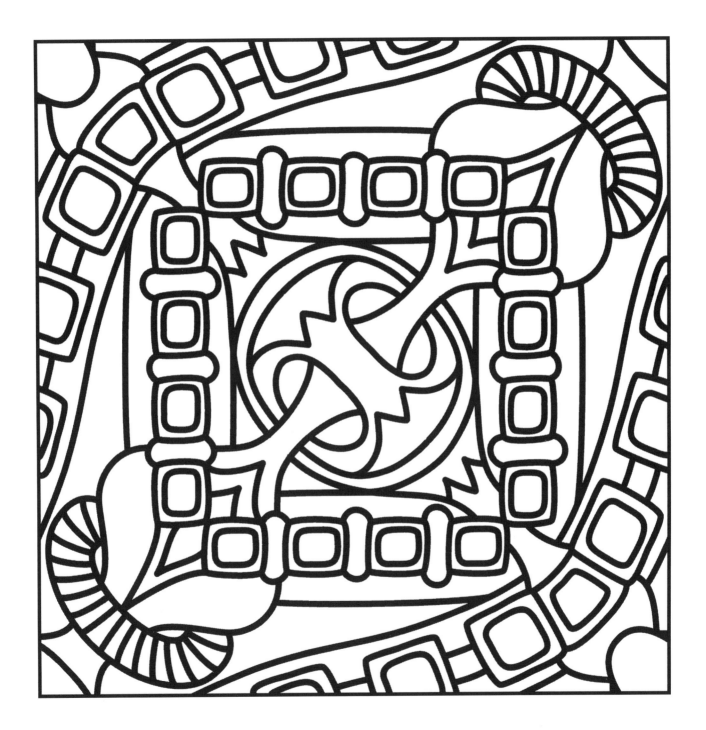

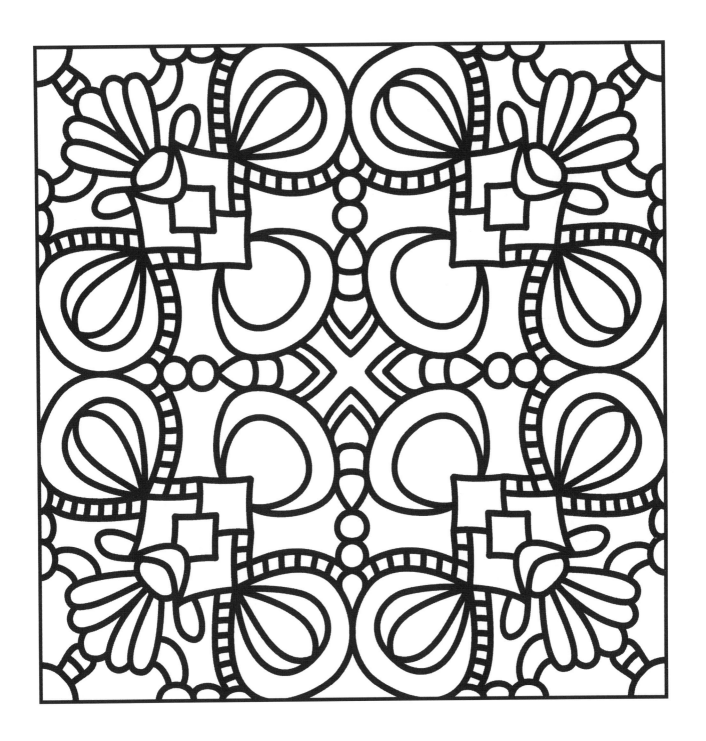

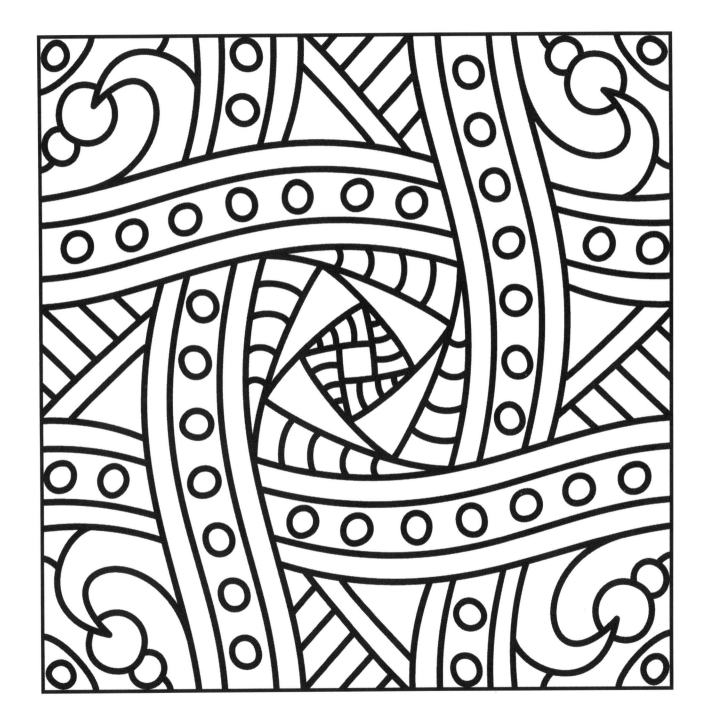

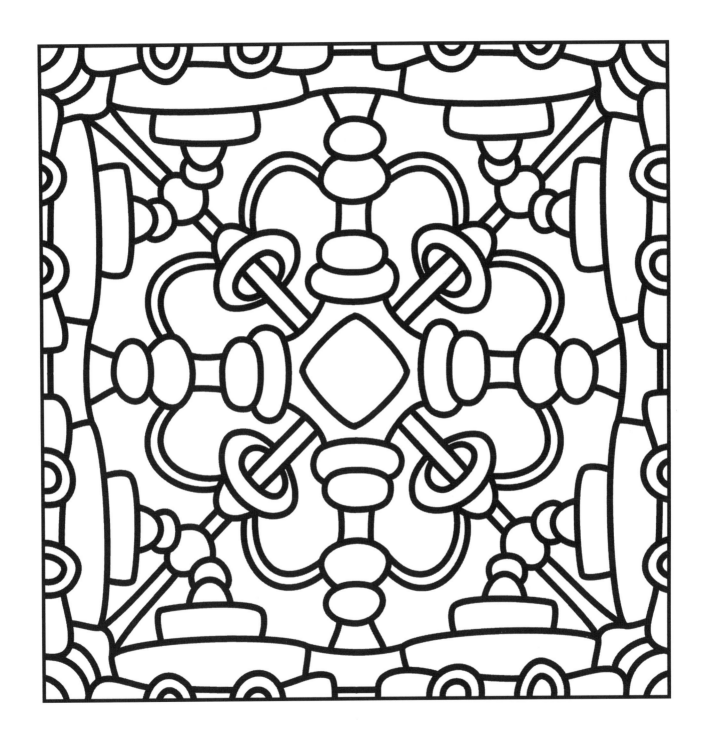

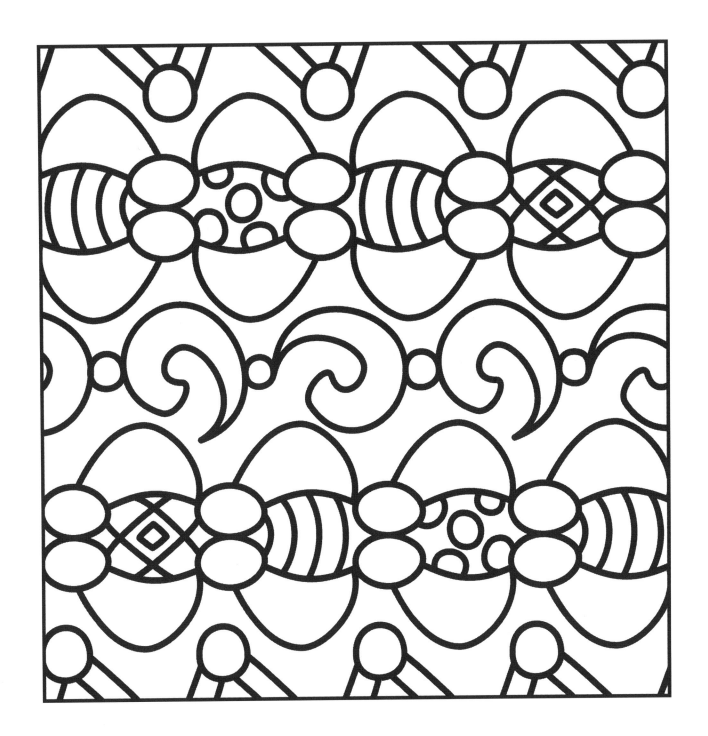

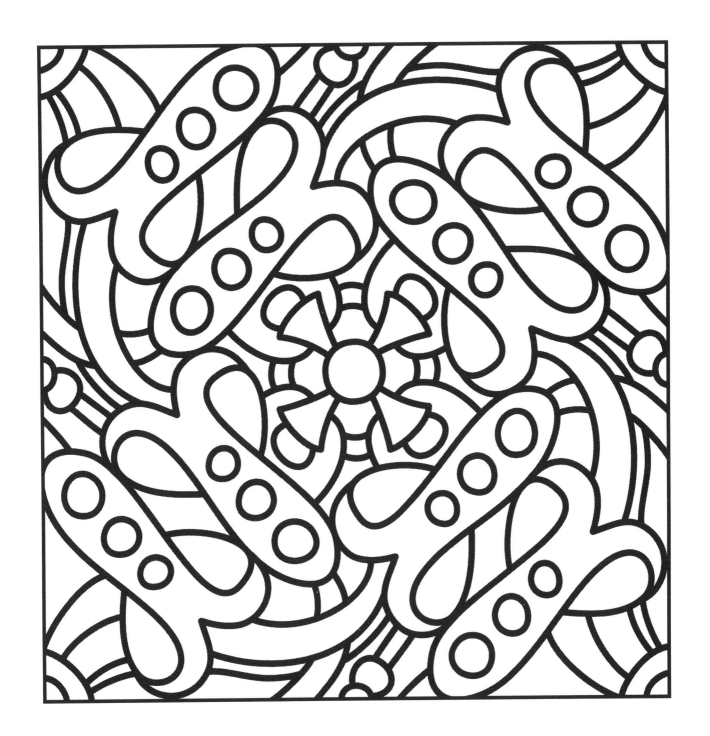

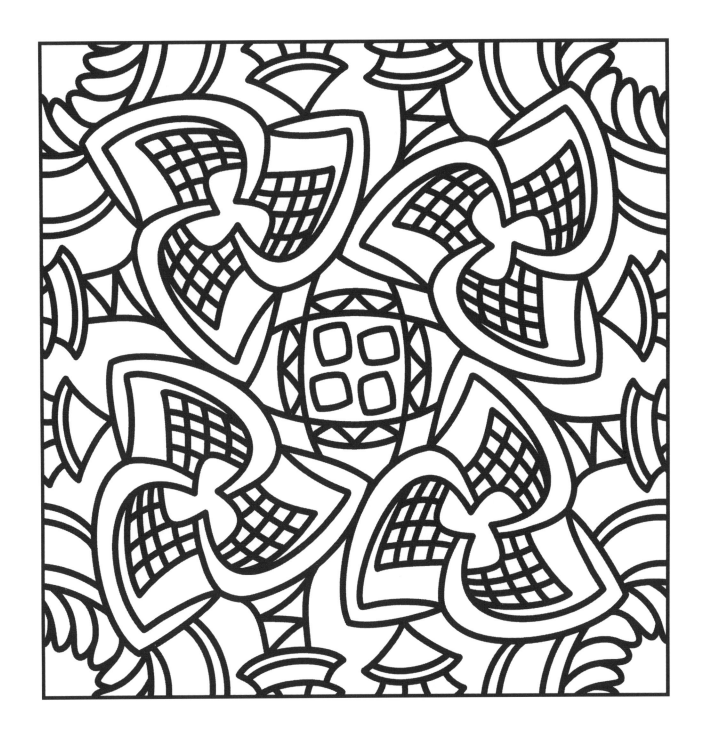

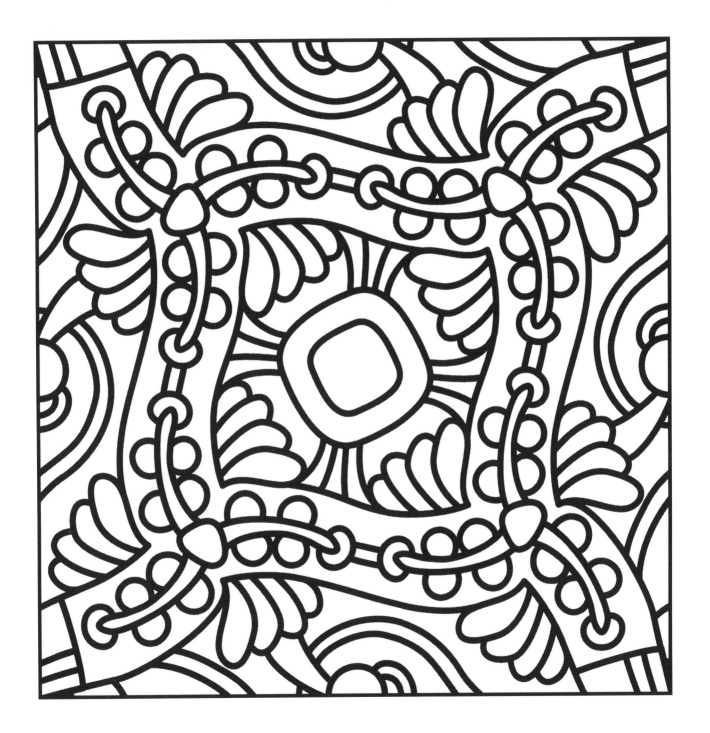

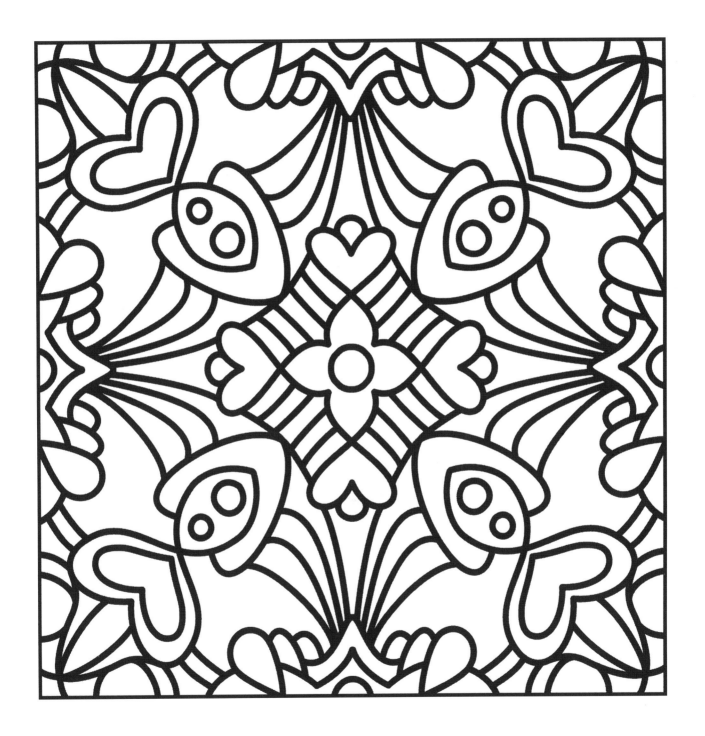

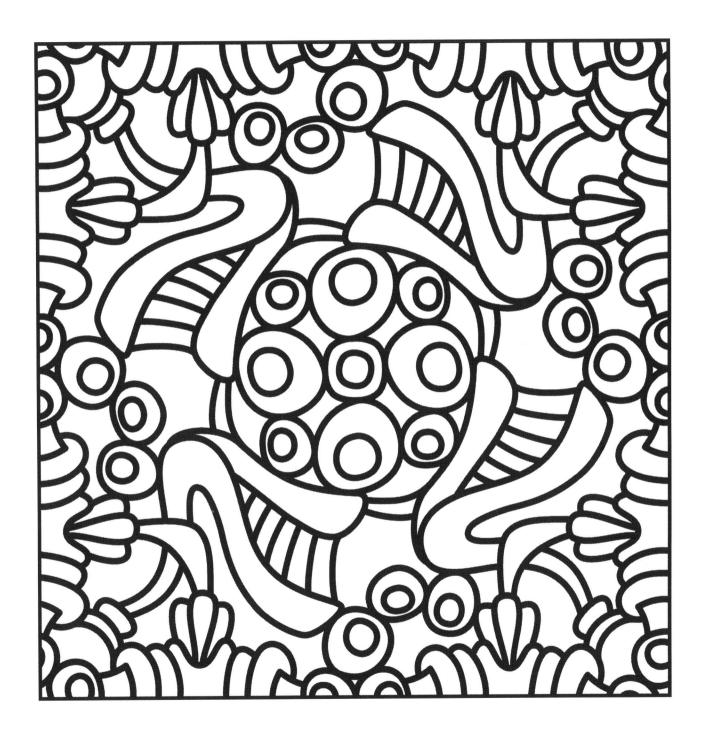

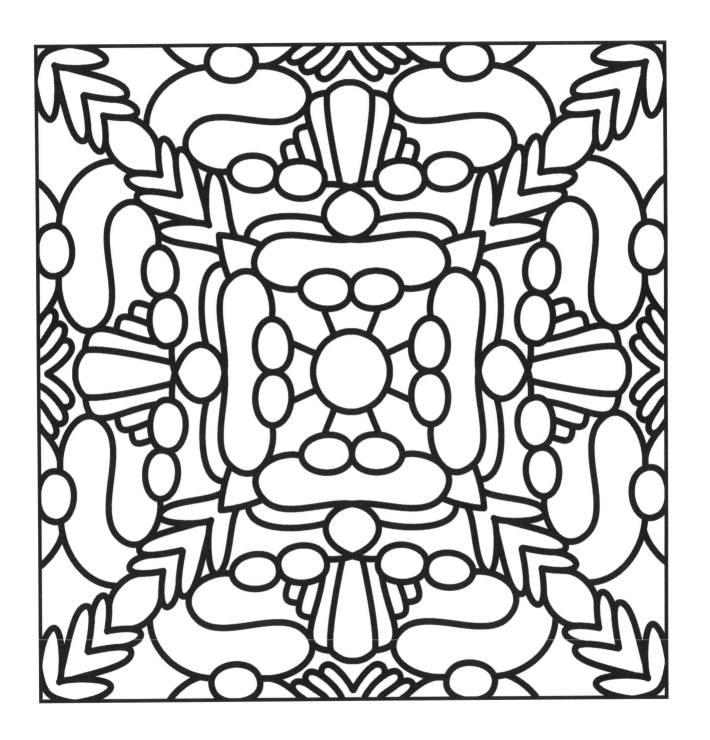

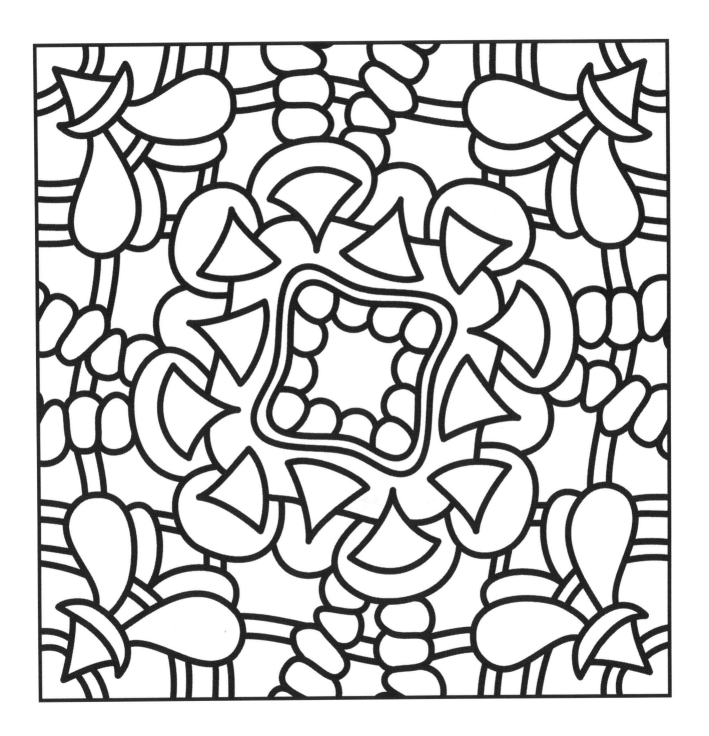

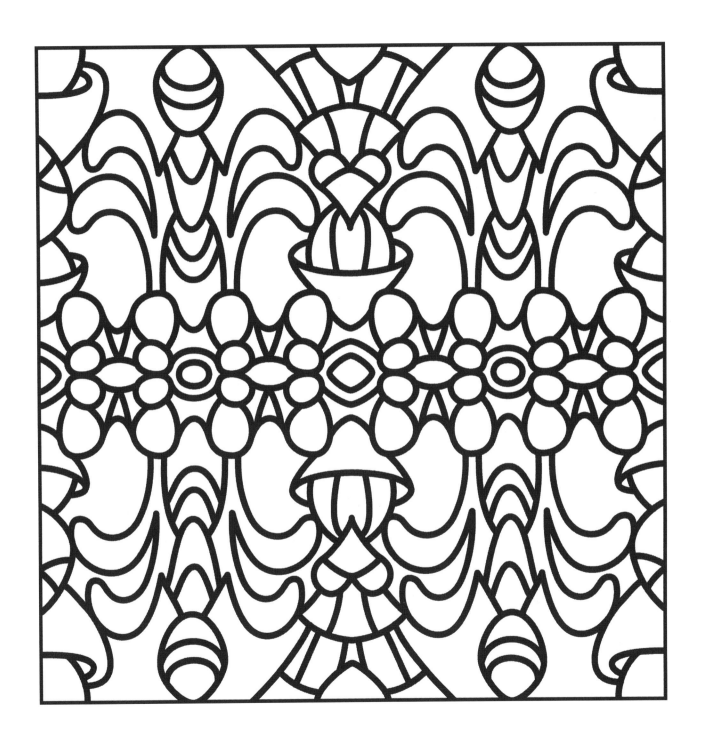

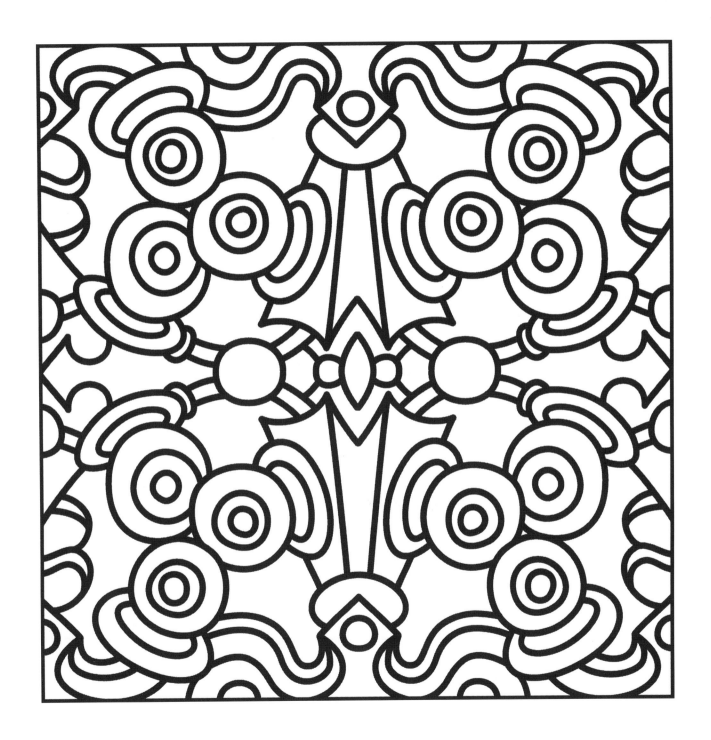

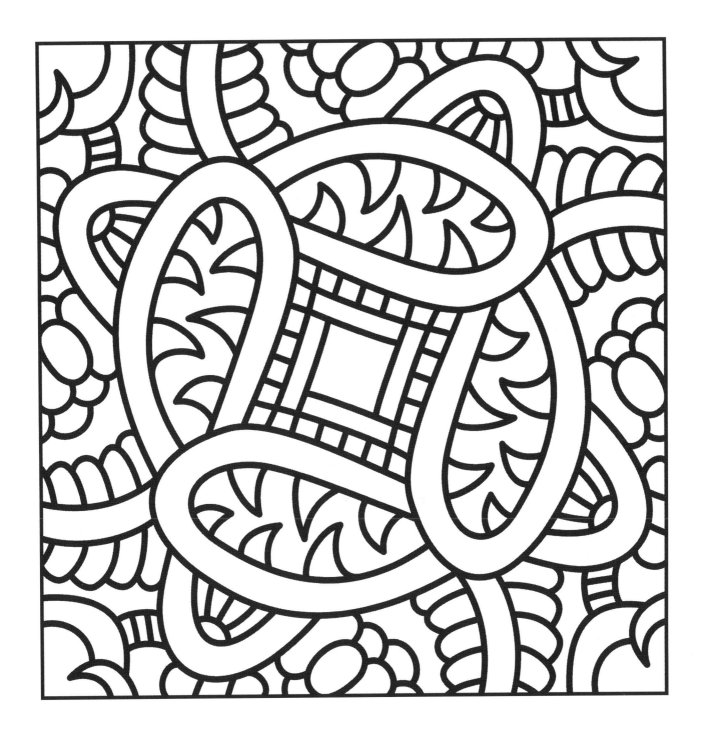

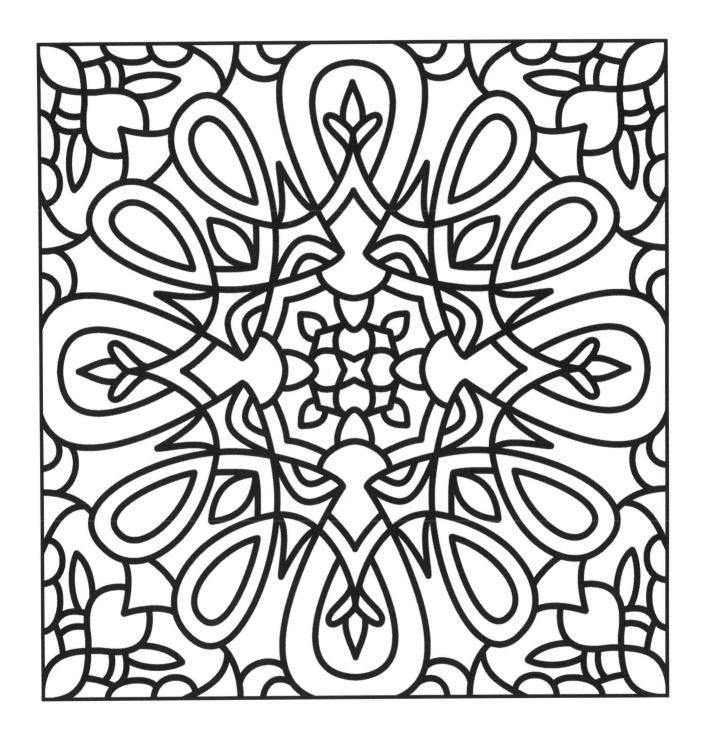

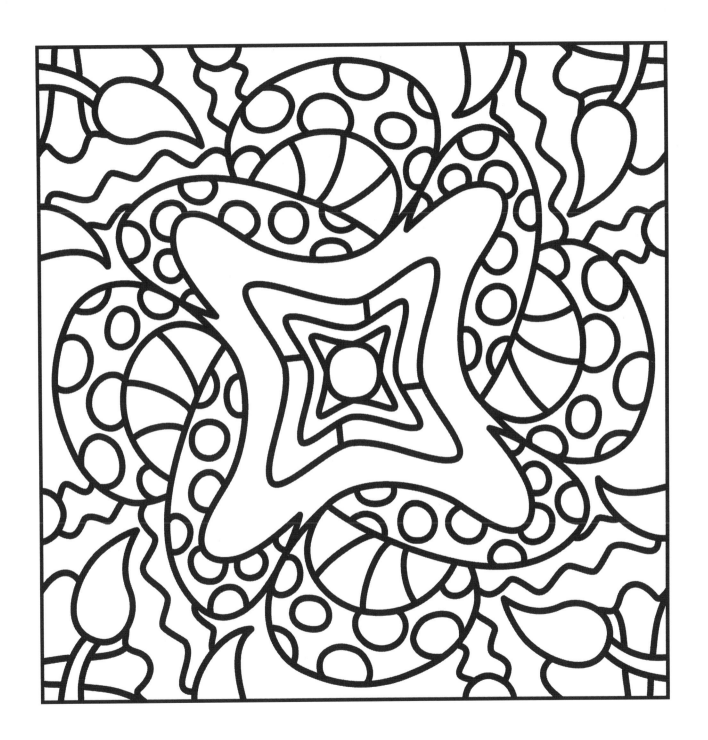

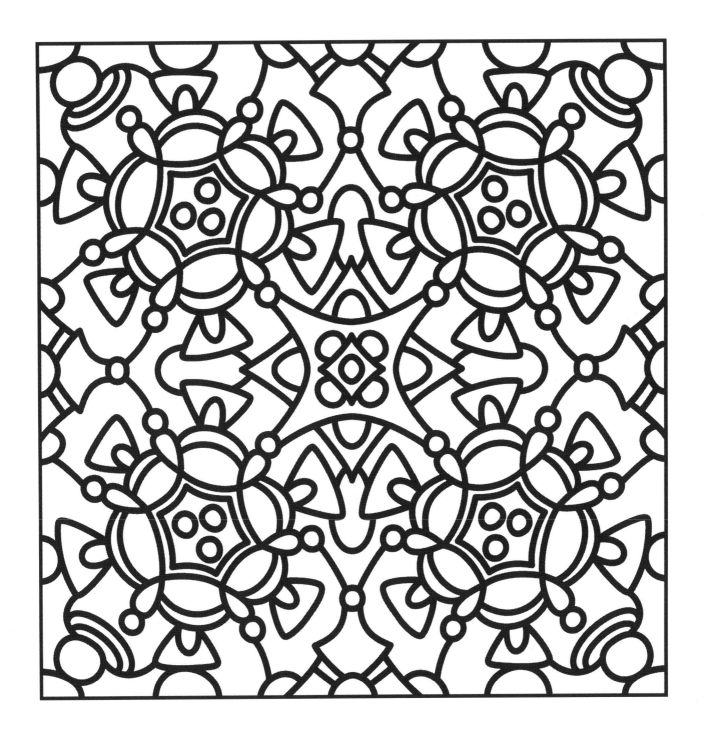

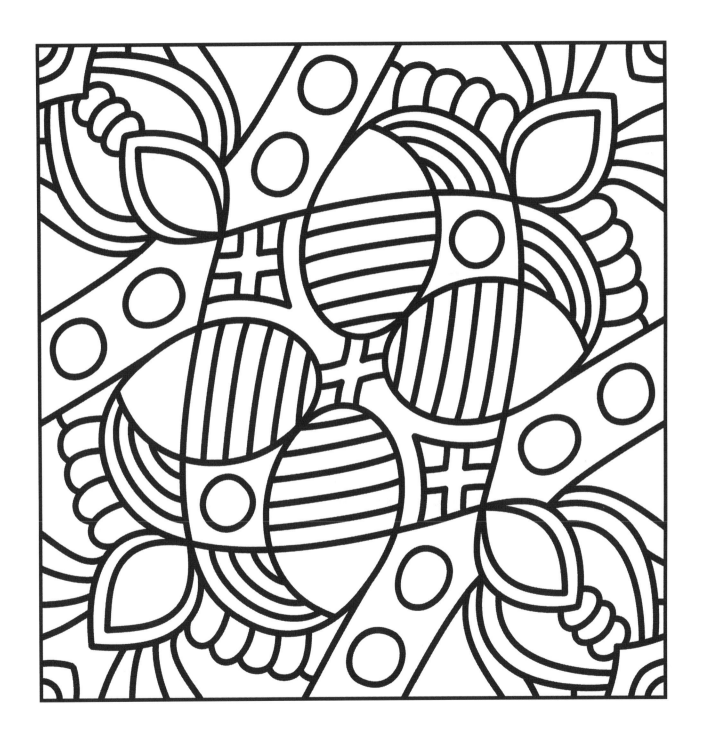

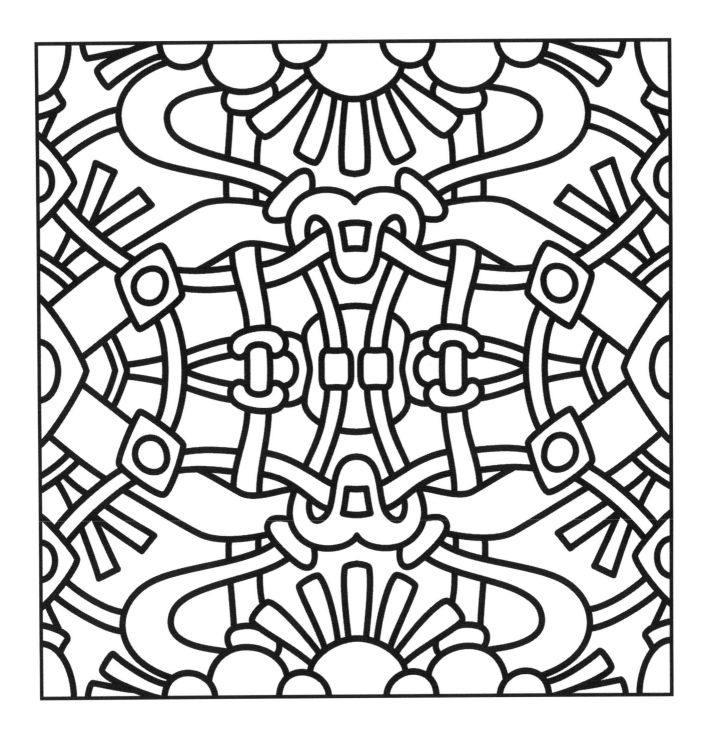

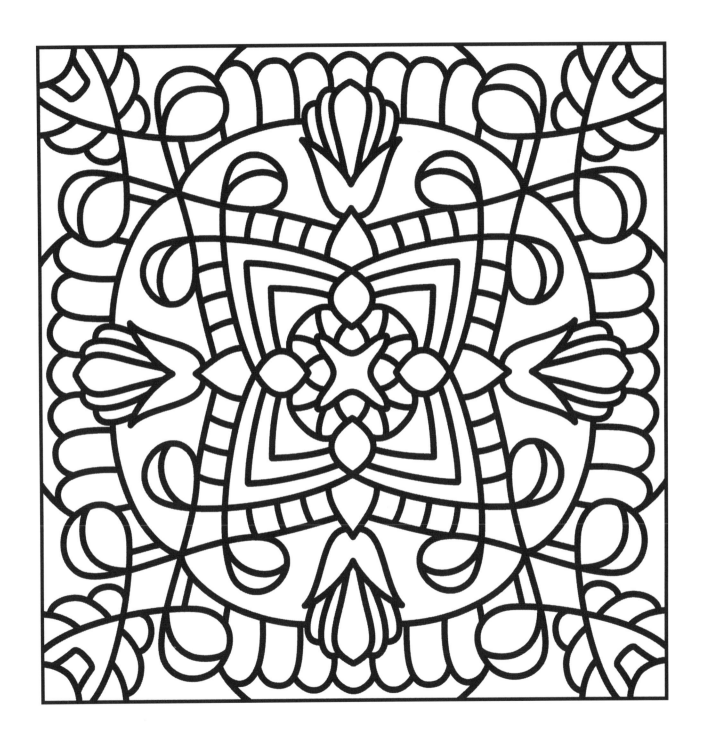

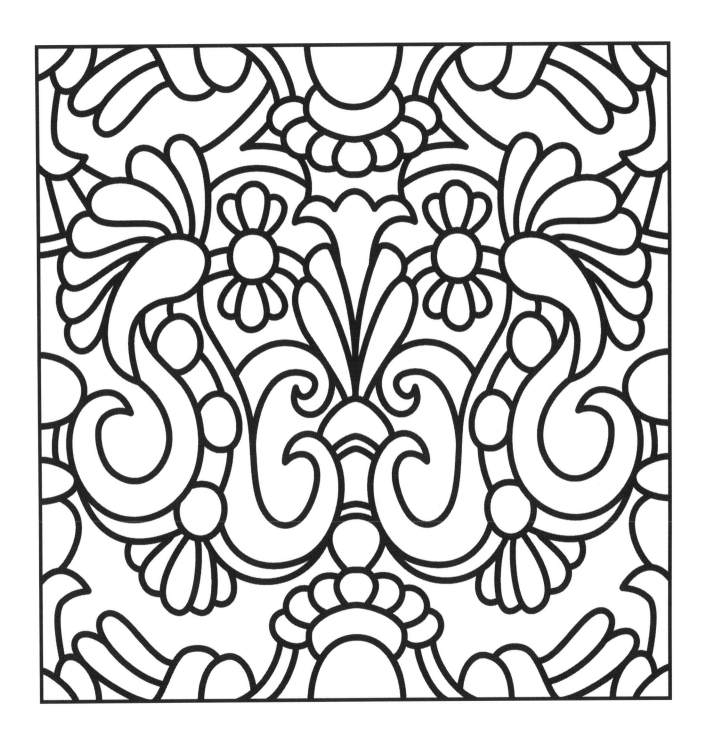

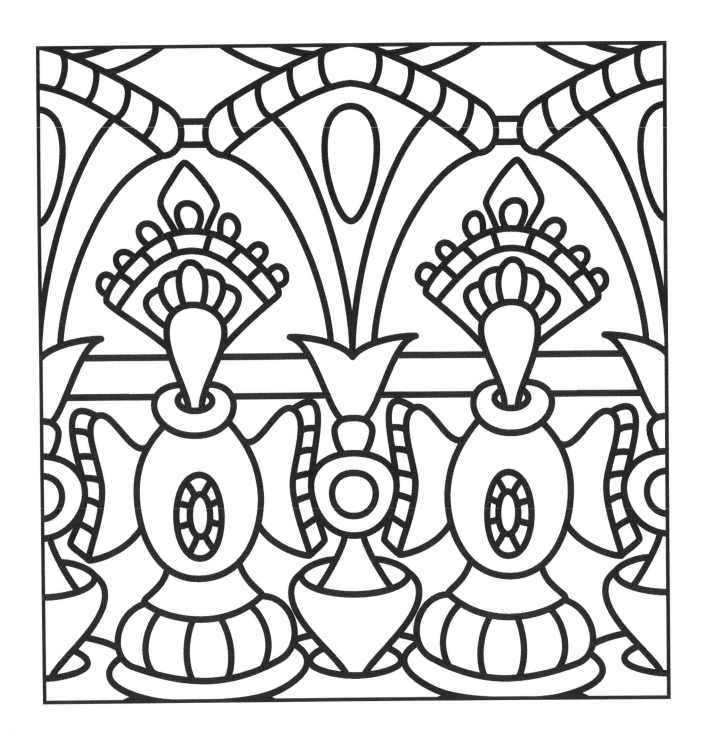

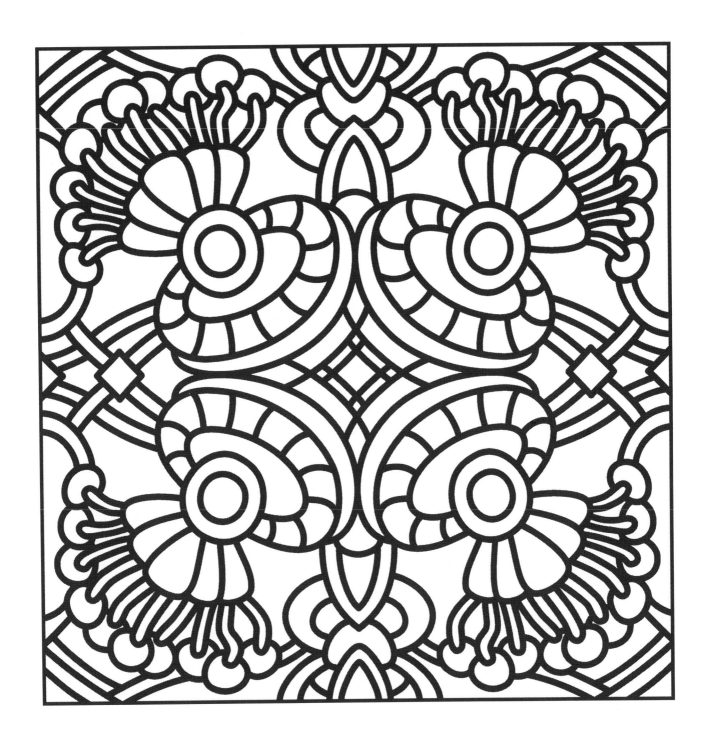

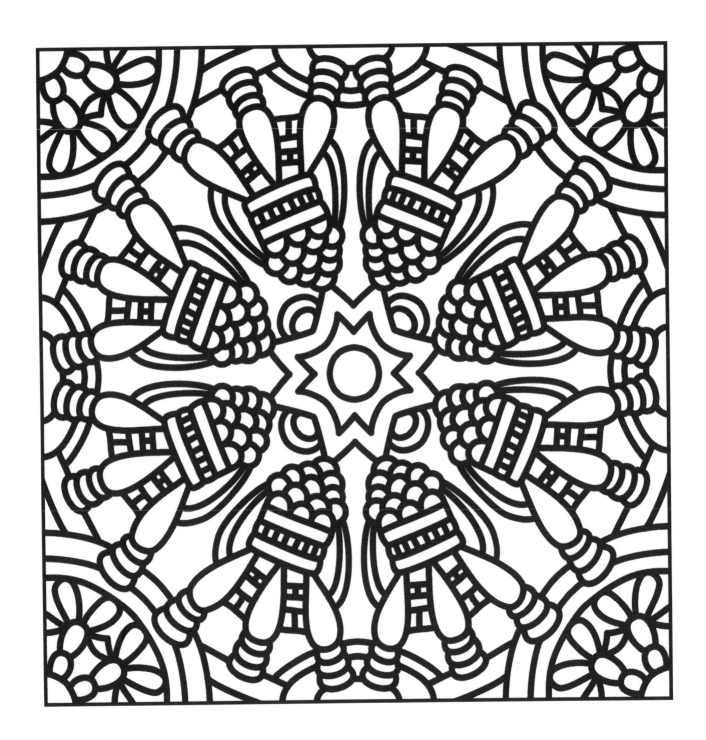

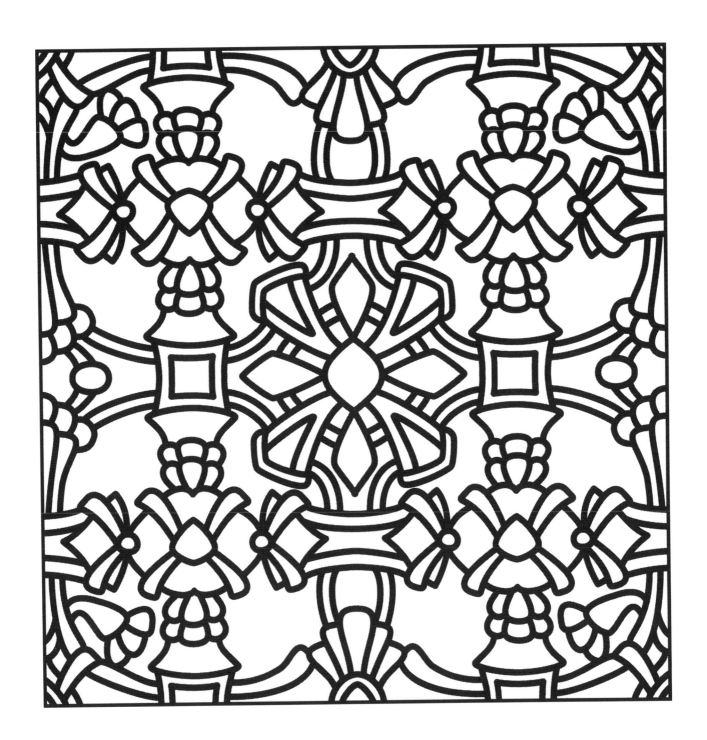

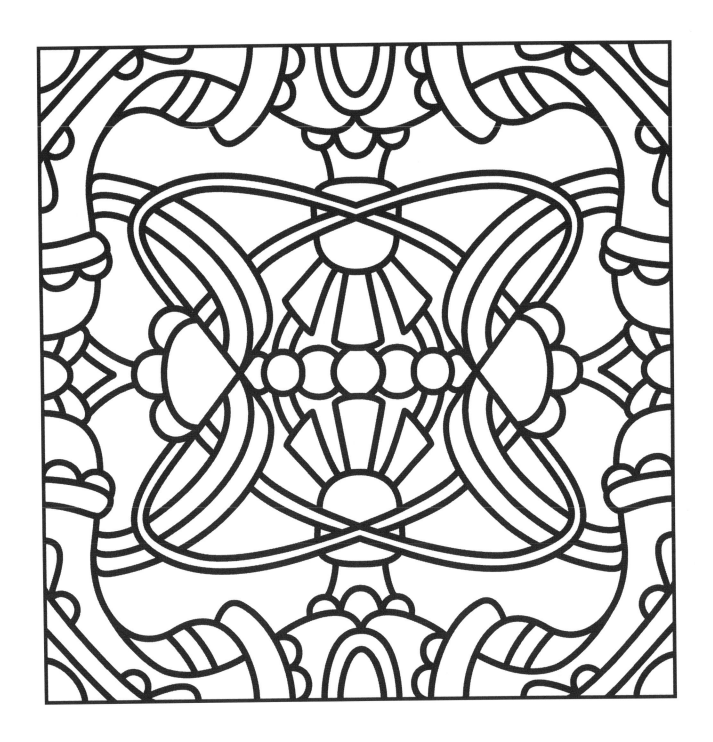

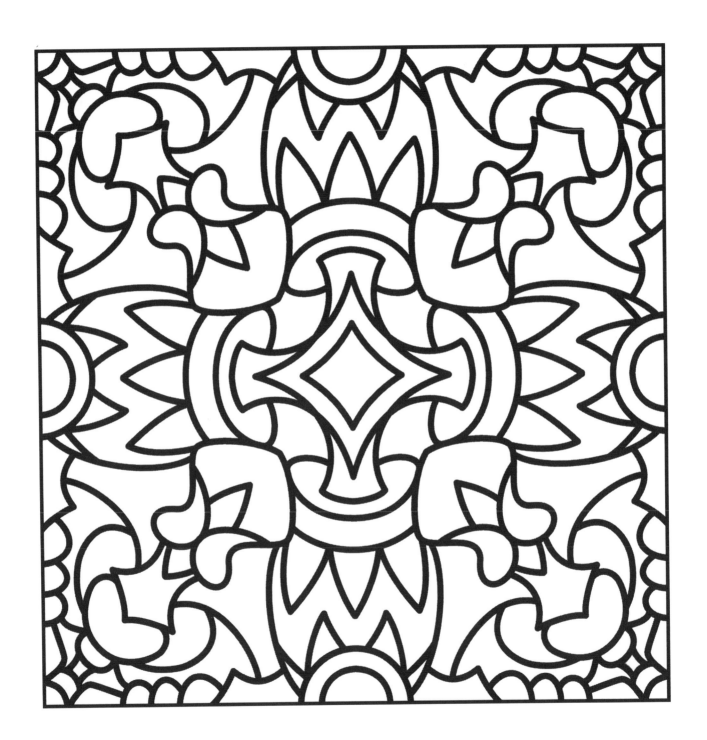

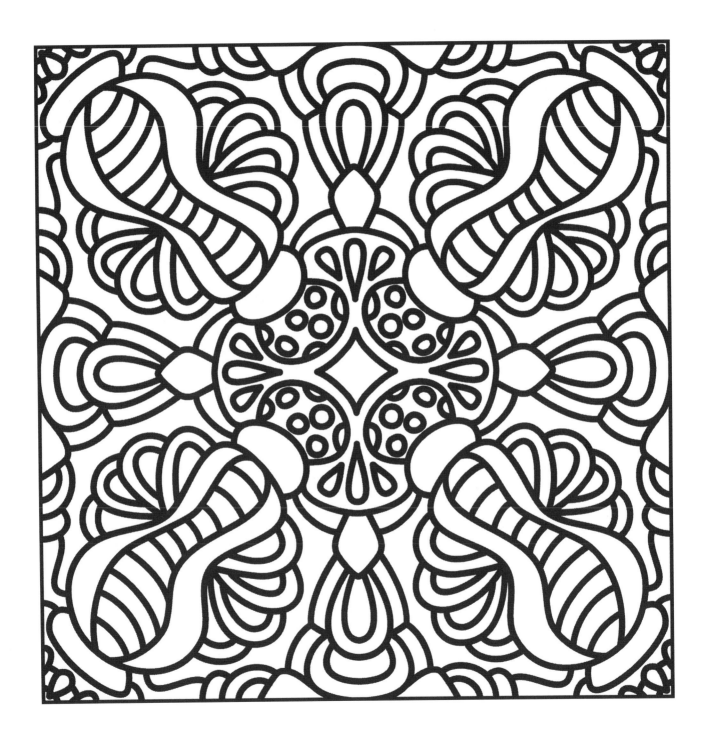

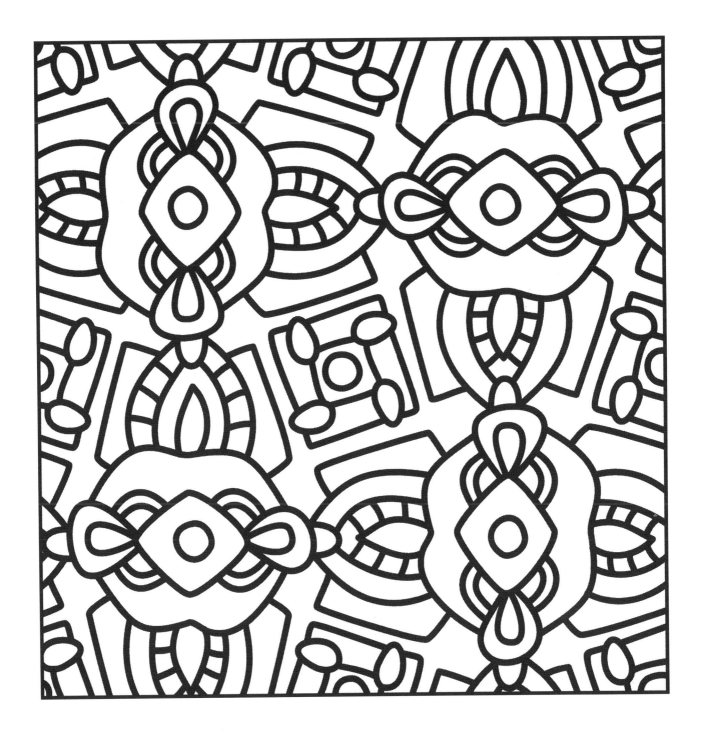

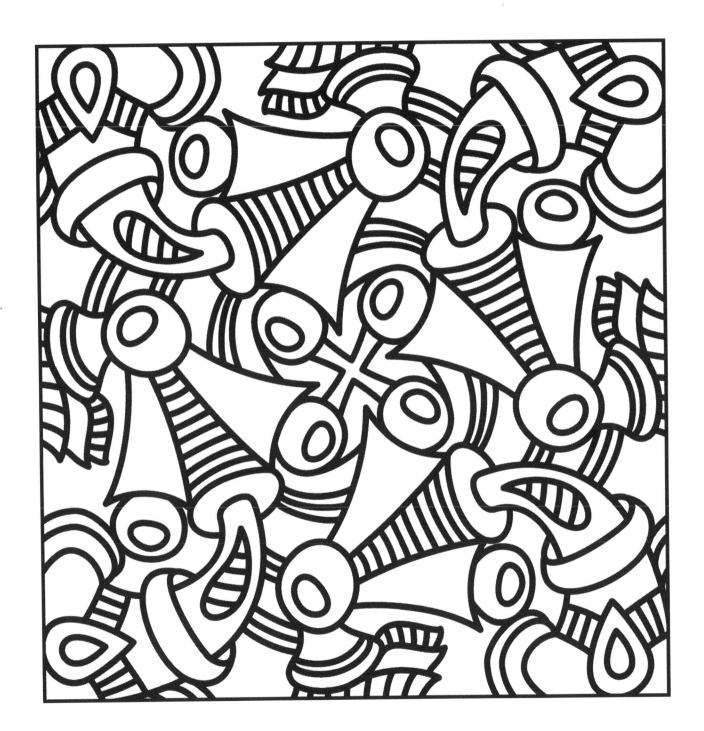

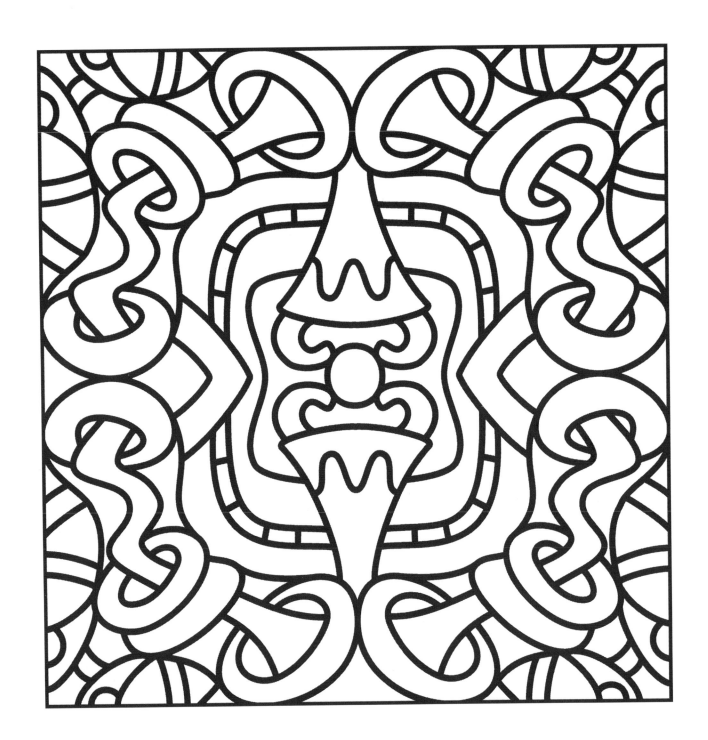

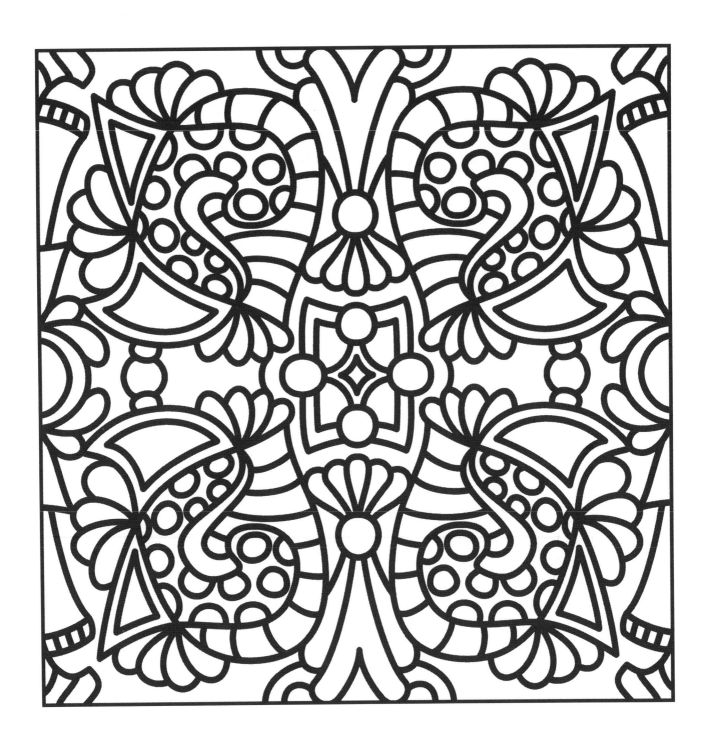

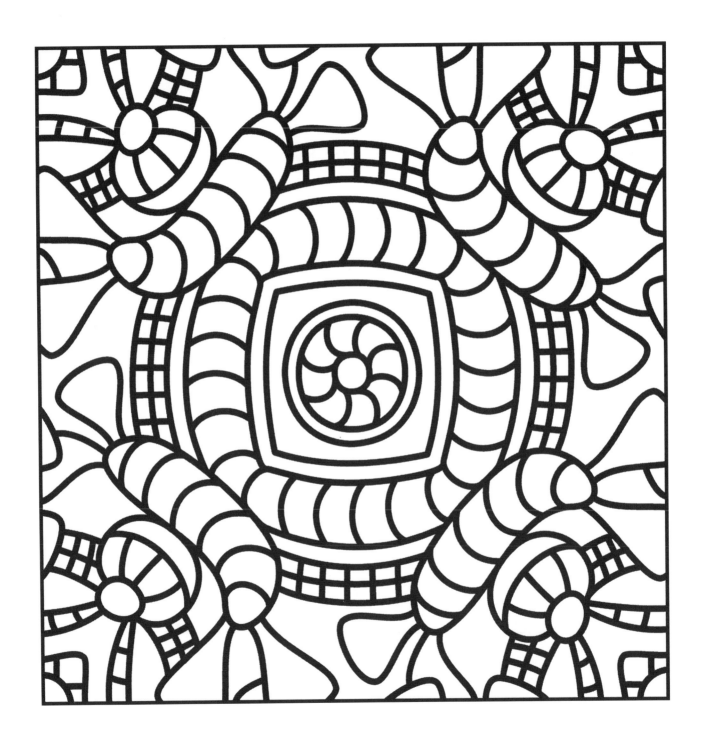

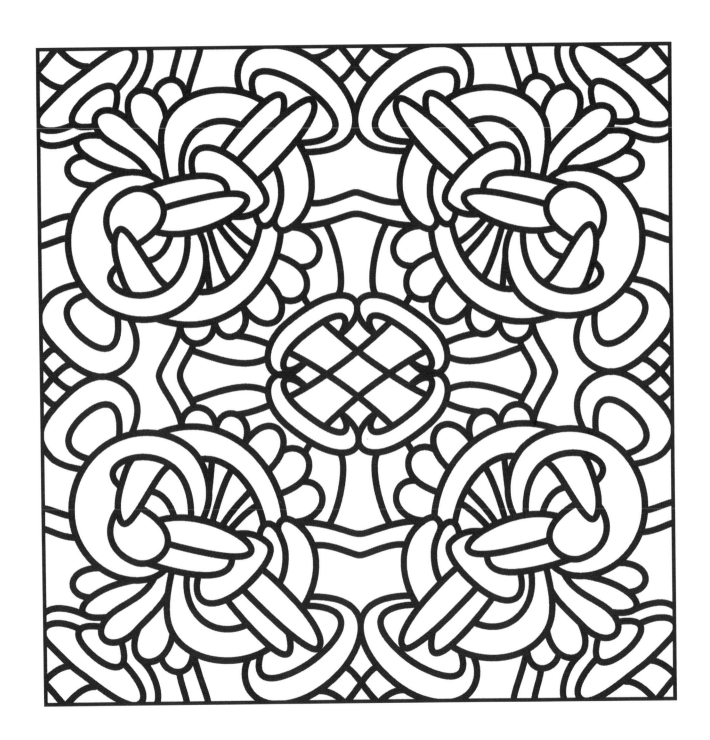

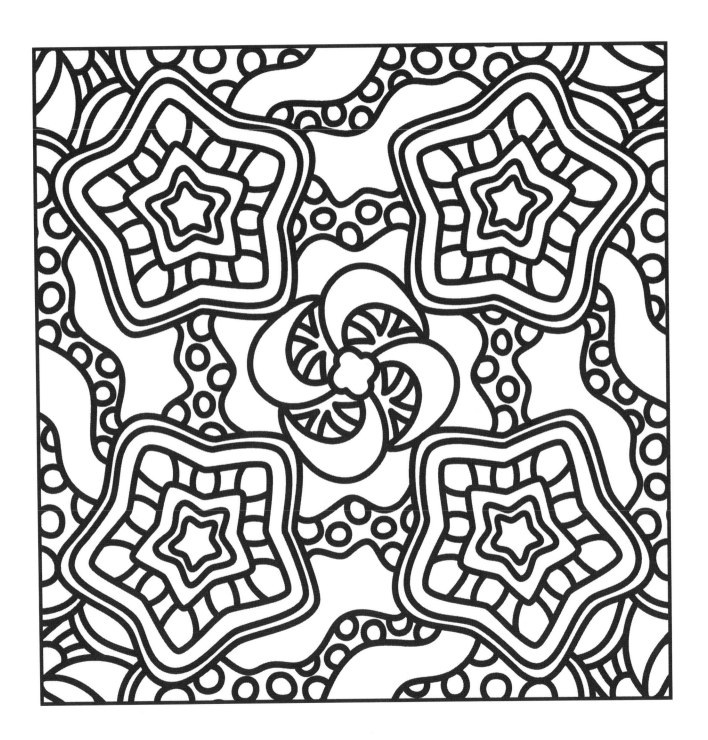

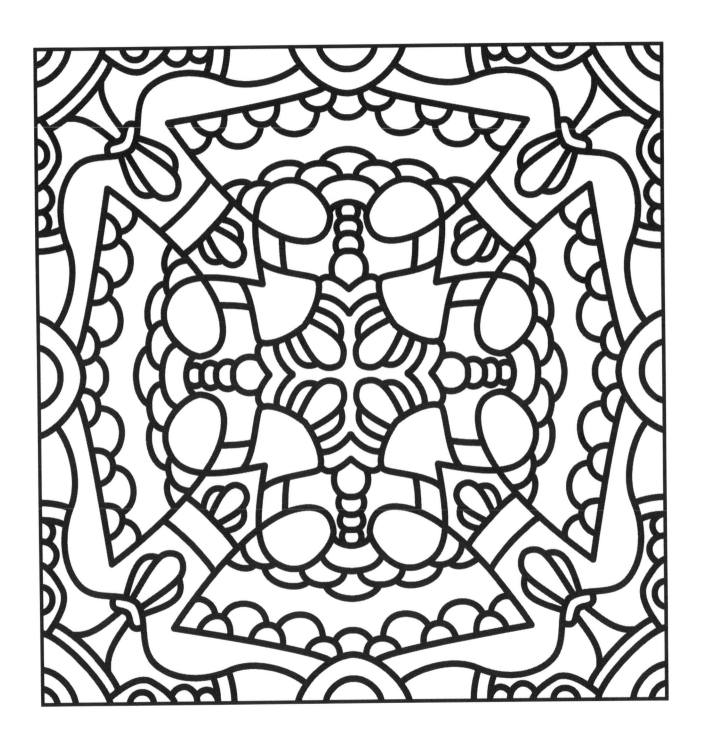

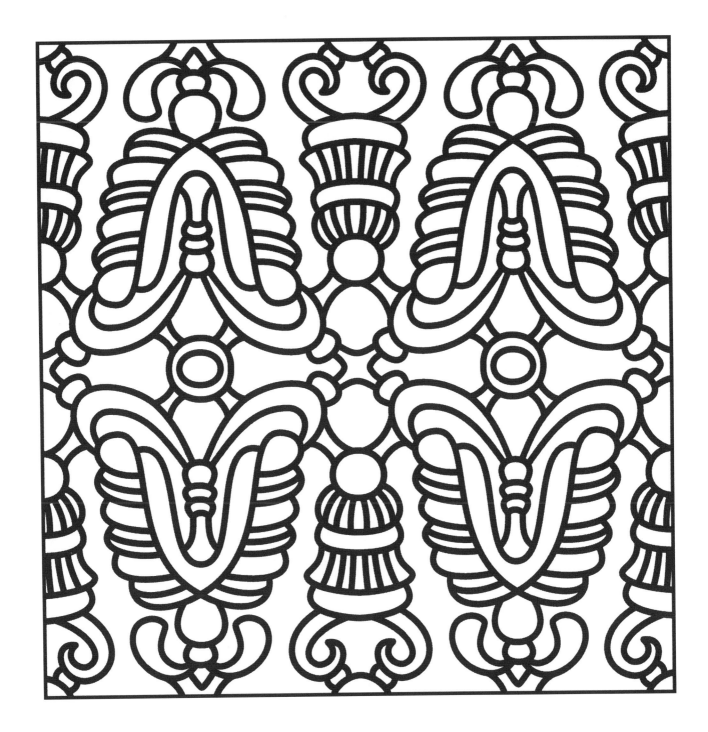

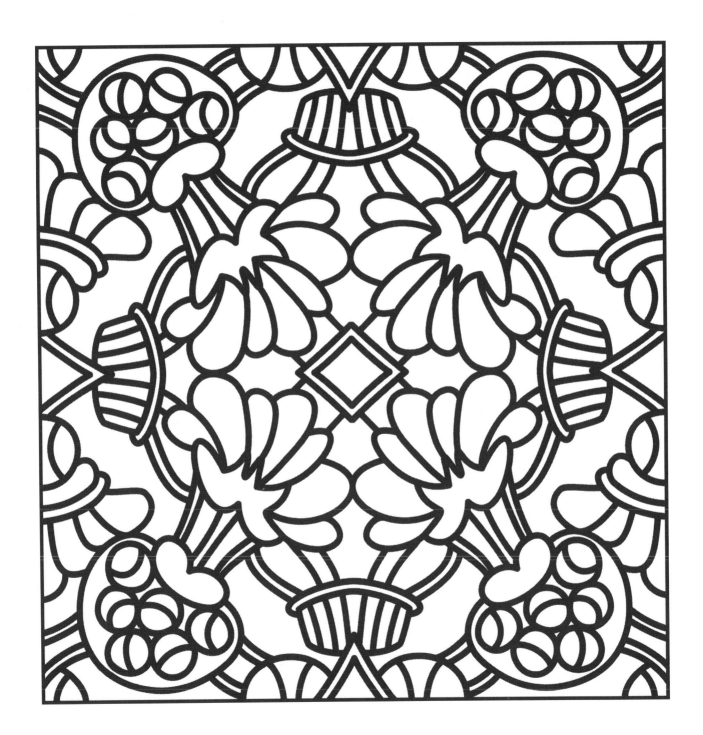

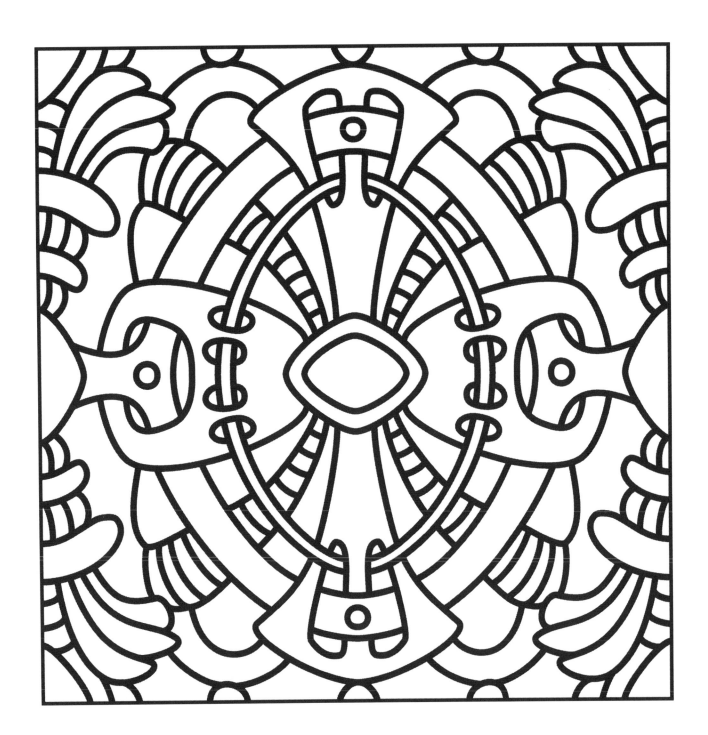

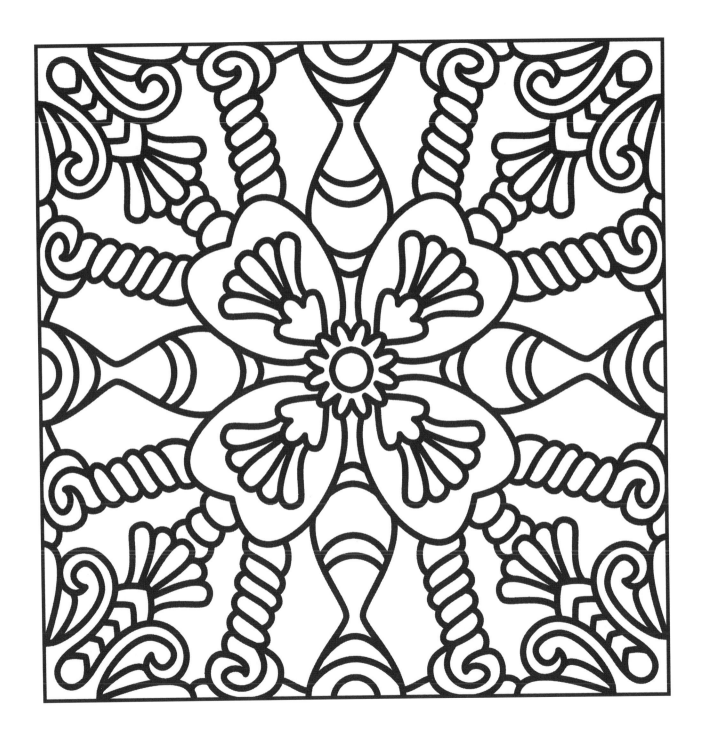

Color With Angie & Friends

Join our friendly Color With Angie Grace Facebook group!

www.AngieGrace.com

Visit Angie's website for special web exclusives for colorists.